THE BELL'S
SEASONING STORY

William G. Bell and the
New England Classic He Created

by David N. Bell

The Firefly Press

Fairhaven, Massachusetts
United States of America

ISBN: 1885553137
ISBN-13: 978-1885553133

DEDICATION

This little book is dedicated to Kathleen and the
Wonder Bunch, whose constant love, support,
humor, joys and challenges sustain me and keep
me young.

CONTENTS

PREFACE

Some years ago, my wife, Kathleen Burkhalter, challenged me to name my eight great-grandparents. I could not, and it got me thinking about the tremendous genetic diversity that courses through each of us. Think of it: we are equally related to each of our 8 great-grandparents, 16 great-great-grandparents, 32 (g)(g)great-grandparents, and so forth back through the generations.

One of Kathleen's cousins in Georgia told us that her grandmother used to ask people she met, "Who are you some of?" which was meant to delve into the rich trove of ancestors whose names we don't carry. Yet, it is common to pay the most attention to the family characters and history (a) of the surname we carry, and/or (b) whose notoriety and stories are passed down in family lore. In my family, William G. Bell has been such a character, as has the history of the company that bears his name.

This book tells the story of William and his company, as illuminated by family lore and papers. However, everyone is some of so many others, and I attempt to introduce as many as possible of those who contributed to the life events I describe in these pages.

Another feature of the book is that, for the most part, it tells about public and business-related events rather than private and family matters. The reason for this is simple: my primary source material is the scrapbook that William himself kept (which was, to a diminished degree, maintained by his family after his death). These are the topics that dominate the material in his scrapbook.

The scrapbook entries, at least during his lifetime, are almost certainly selected by William himself. This makes them a combination of sentimental (about family things), proud (about accomplishments), and humorous (about things at which he pokes fun - including adversaries and himself). There are hints of sanctimony, but almost nothing of anger or aggression.

Although these biographical vignettes are not meant to present an impartial or balanced picture of William's life, they are remarkably open to rich interpretation. For example, along with factual articles describing the family firm's bankruptcy in 1890, an event that must have been among the most traumatic and humiliating of his life, William includes an editorial that crows, "It may interest butchers throughout the country to learn that the head of the firm of William G. Bell & Co. is another one of those sanctimonious Sunday-school gentlemen who so frequently appear in bad odor in the commercial sphere. The creditors are evidently paying for the church contributions this time." And attached next to a glowing letter of adulation about the unblemished excellence of his company's culture is a rambling tantrum from an employee about an internecine "cat fight."

Whether or not he intended it, the clues

unambiguously outline the man and the business that is so much a personification of the man. He was industrious, persistent, energetic, egalitarian, generous, sanctimonious, anti-Catholic in some things, tee totaling, exacting, and in small measure, quirky – in short, a classic Yankee. And the company that he labored to build and save and build again remains, one hundred fifty-two years later, a Yankee classic.

INTRODUCTION

At 6 a.m. on Saturday, December 31, 2011, Kathleen, daughter, Ana-Maria, and I left our home in New Bedford, Mass. on a 150-mile drive to Laconia, New Hampshire. Earlier that week, in a quiet moment between Christmas and New Year festivities, we had been alerted to an auction of family items that would take place on that day. We were startled to find, among the photographs of listed items, a number of heirlooms that were icons of Bell family history.

There was irony in the date: it was the last day of the 150th anniversary of the year in which the William G. Bell Co., inventor and purveyor of the New England classic Bell's Spiced Seasoning, was founded. The company and its story has been a central feature of our family identity, and some items in the catalog held ties to characters in the story. Was this to be some kind of cosmic last hurrah? Kathleen, Ana-Maria and I were determined to change that fate.

We arrived at the auction house, secured our bidder's number, and cased the floor. The family items leapt out at us. It felt like they were calling to us plaintively, like orphans. With a mix of dread and urgency, we steeled ourselves for the bidding, which began at 10 a.m., and plunged into the fray. For the next five hours, we wielded our placard, number 86, with ferocious tenacity and waged pitched battles with dealers, absentee bidders, and determined collectors.

In the end, we were successful. Our small sedan, filled to bursting with precious treasures, like an automotive piñata, turned south in the gloaming and aimed for New Bedford. We carried back with us all we needed for the next chapter in the family story.

The story of the William G. Bell Co. is one of "push, pluck and principle," as described by a contemporary. It is a success story: not of a titan of industry from a background of Brahmin privilege, but, rather, a resourceful, determined, and entrepreneurial son of New England soil. It is an amalgam of hard work, eccentricities, criss-crossing fortunes, and characters within and without the web of blood relations; it holds secrets and suspense, sadness and joy; it weaves together names that charm and tantalize - Fair Helen of Kirkconnel, Colonel Prescott, Perlmutter from Palestine, and Douglas Crook.

Here it is in a nutshell. A border clan in Scotland ends up on the wrong side of the crown. They emigrate for the newly formed Ulster Plantations in Ireland and, after two generations, join the momentous Scots-Irish migration to America. Bells thrive on New Hampshire soil until some decide to take a chance in the big city of Boston. Along the way, the great blending of blood lines joins Bells with Bruces, Whitneys, Goldsmiths, Storys,

Stoughtons, Parkers, and Johnsons. A business is born in the bustling streets and markets of Boston. A brand is born in the infancy of a national holiday. Families grow and the business prospers. No life is without its share of hardship and misfortune, and a hallmark of character is the comeback from adversity. Prosperity, expansion, weddings, golden years follow. There is a big house on a hill from which a prominent family radiates confidence and success. And, suddenly, the lights go dark...

After a slumber of generations, we return to tell the story. We are rested, with fresh legs and new blood, reaching back and ready to carry the baton forward.

CHAPTER 1

The Story Begins

In his autobiographical notes, William G. Bell writes, "Began work for Mr. McGuffy, Lowell, Mass., 1850. Age 11 years. Worked six months at $1 per week." Thus begins a life of work that would not cease until William's death sixty-five years later. Private letters, business correspondence, and articles all repeat the refrain of his tireless energy, good spirits and fairness. In the same notebook, William continues his narrative of industry. "At 12 years of age I prevailed upon my father to let me leave school to work in the market of Mr. Gilbert." He accumulates a bookkeeping certificate from the Commercial College of Mr. McCoy and dives back into a merchant's life.

Although his early experiences are almost all within the food markets of Lowell, one entrepreneurial foray stands out. On June 28, 1856, the City of Lowell granted a license to William G. Bell "to keep and sell fireworks from the 28th day of June till the fourth day of July, inclusive." Two days later, a receipt is issued from Mills & Forristall, Importers, Wholesale and Retail Dealers in Clocks, Watches, Jewelry, Cutlery, Toys and Fancy Goods of every description, No. 42 Faneuil Hall Square to W. G. Bell in the amount of $38.47 (or, about $900 today). The receipt itemizes 12 boxes of crackers, 1 box of Roman Candles, 1 box of Flower Pots, 1 box of Torpedoes, 1 box of Bengal Lights, and diverse other fireworks. It is marked "Paid" in the elegant quill-inked script of the day and signed by Mr. Forristall himself. It must have been a festive and profitable 4th of July. William was 17 years old. The holiday money-making spark was lit.

CHAPTER 2

The House on 49 Shaw Street

New Year's Day, January 1, 1914. The Boston Budget and Beacon reports:

A brilliant wedding took place in West Newton on New Year's, when Douglass Crook and Marian Bell, daughter of Mr. and Mrs. William G. Bell, were married at the home of the bride on Shaw Street. The bride was charming in a gown of white crepe meteor, trimmed with princess lace. She wore a veil and orange blossoms and carried a shower bouquet of white roses...The floral decorations...all suggested the Christmas season...and were surpassingly beautiful. The special feature was a huge arch in the front drawing-room window where the bridal couple stood during the reception...At either side of the arch, in the recess afforded by a huge bay window, was a graceful Christmas tree, 10 feet high...The grand staircase was a mass of green festoons and the balustrade was interwoven with white satin ribbon...[T]he same charming decorations were seen in every room of the spacious Bell residence wherever a window, arched recess or chandelier gave the opportunity.

West Newton, a village of Newton, lies west of Boston not far from the meandering path of the Charles River. As the bird flies, its village center is less than ten miles from the Commercial Street and Quincy Market locations of the Bell family enterprises. According to historian Diana Muir, West Newton is one of America's original commuter suburbs. The Boston and Worcester railroad reached West Newton in 1834. Gracious homes sprang up almost instantly on erstwhile farmland on West Newton hill, as men wealthy enough to afford a country seat, but whose business demanded that they be in their downtown Boston offices during the business day, took advantage of the new commuting opportunity offered by the railroad. Muir points out that these early commuters needed sufficient wealth to employ a groom and keep horses, to drive them from their hilltop homes to the station.

Shaw Street on West Newton Hill runs roughly north to south, no more than a quarter mile from West Newton Square. From Washington Street, it rises steeply and terminates at Winthrop Street. 49 Shaw Street dominates the southwest corner of Shaw and Winthrop Streets at the top of the hill. It commands a view to points northwest, north, and northeast and takes in the gentle river valley of the Charles, the dusky hills of Waltham, and the lofty spire of the Second Congregational Church.

The house, built around 1870, is in the Colonial Revival style with Victorian embellishments. Its three floors rise proudly in keeping with the prominence of its post at the crown of the hill. The foundation is nearly 50 feet square, with an appendage housing the kitchen and maids' rooms jutting an additional twenty-five feet west from the rear of the house. The square hipped roof is punctuated by two double-windowed dormers on each of three sides. An expansive wrap-around porch begins at the front entrance and forms a sweeping half-moon around the north-facing side of the house. Commanding the slope of the hill as it does, it takes on the character of the bow of a great ship whose captain can survey vast swaths from its decks. Bay windows and textured scrollwork on the porch and window peaks add to the home's appearance of ample self-satisfaction.

Today, one can hear the dull swish of cars on the Massachusetts Turnpike. In William's time, it was the train line, the Boston and Worcester, which would have provided the intrusion of modern technology upon the tranquil scene. The neighborhood remains abundantly green, with stately, old maple, ash, oak and pine trees, many of which might have been saplings when William's grandchildren gamboled in the yard. It is easy to imagine William briskly climbing the hill on a summer evening, making his way back from another day in the city, mind engaged, perhaps, in the next day's tasks and opportunities. Inside, as dusk approached, meal preparations would be well under way, and Yankee sense of propriety and order being as they are, family would be preparing for dinner.

By 1914, the year of Marian Bell's marriage, 49 Shaw Street would have been home to three generations: Mary (Whitney) Bell and William, daughter, Marian, son, Alfred, his wife, Hattie Gertrude (Johnson), and their children, Dorothy, William, Alfred, and Douglas. Along with a modest house staff, these nine gave life to the walls.

CHAPTER 3

A New Hampshire Boyhood

Perhaps it was the Scottish stock – Bruces, Campbells, and Wilsons among those clans from whom he was descended – or perhaps the country soil in southern New Hampshire, but whatever the source, the instinct for hard work and industry seemed to emerge from the womb with William. Family members and friends recall him as being earnest and busy. A school teacher reminisces, "You were six when you first came to me and what a painstaking, conscientious little fellow!"

According to family records, little Billy was a bundle of enterprise from an early age.

Between the ages of four and nine he kept hens, raised squashes, saved ashes for the soap man, raked tan for his father's tannery, gathered herbs, and tended the neighbors' cows.

One tale bears witness to little Billy's business instincts. Once, when the minister went away, Billy was asked to drive his cow to pasture. Before the minister's return, Billy asked his father what he should charge the man of the cloth. He fidgeted awkwardly at his father's suggestion that he give his services for free. Noticing his son's reaction, Robert Bell advised, "Take it in preaching," which is what little Billy did.

William was born in Hancock, New Hampshire on February 1, 1839. Hancock occupies a swath of land characterized by a quilt of forest and meadow, stitched with stone walls and streams in the Merrimac River watershed in southwest New Hampshire. It lies about 20 miles west of Manchester, 15 miles north of the Massachusetts border, and a similar 20 miles east of the great Connecticut River valley and the border with Vermont.

Hancock was founded in 1754, a generation after the Bells and their kin first settled in the Derry and Londonderry Scotch-Irish communities to the east.

Although the most colorful interpretation of Bell ancestry wends back through John to Matthew of Kirkconnel, Scotland and the famous Border Reiver Clan, a version reinforced by numerous references in family notes and letters, the exact genealogical path back to the old country remains unproven. We do know for certain that William's great-grandfather William was born around 1715 in either Londonderry, New Hampshire or Andover, Massachusetts and married Abigail/Deborah/Sarah Kittredge, of Andover. Together they had eleven children, nine of whom survived to adulthood, including William's grandfather, Hugh, the seventh son. Hugh was born in 1771 in Andover, married Nancy Wilson and had Robert Gibson Bell, William's father. Robert married Sophronia Bruce of Ackworth, New Hampshire.

That is the rudimentary skeleton of Bell genealogy in America. The bones, tissue and blood of their early colonial lives can be found in the stories. There is abundant evidence of family life and death, passed down orally from Hugh to Robert to William, who transcribed for posterity. The story begins with war.

By 1750, the population of the English colonies in America had passed one million. However, it was spread out from Maine to South Carolina and the vast majority of it clung to the seaboard for both livelihood and security. Only three cities - Philadelphia, New York and Boston - could boast populations over 15,000. Hamlets, villages and towns were scattered like seeds north and west of the coastal centers. Yet, what must have given the appearance of pastoral tranquility actually disguised a turbulent and violent instability.

The surging tide of English colonists encroached inexorably on native tribal lands, sovereignty, cultural and economic survival. It also pressed strenuously against French territorial claims in the Americas, which ran to the north and west of English colonial territories. The first rupture occurred in 1675, when the King Philip's War embroiled New

England. It seemed that a nearly unbroken chain of violent struggle would follow in the 18th century, including the Queen Anne's War, Dummer's War, King George's War and the French and Indian War, culminating in the American Revolution, fought largely on America's vast frontiers. Into this cauldron of violence fell generations of farmers and their sons.

The legacy, below, originated with Hugh Bell. It was passed to his son, Robert, and so on, so that my grandfather, William, recounting it almost verbatim, passed it on to me, the great-great-great-great-great-grandson of the first American William.

My grandfather, William Bell, was born in America. He was in the French War (I think he died before I was born) in the English Army...He was taken to Canada as a prisoner of the Indians and made a slave of. He was thought a good deal of as he was a slave to the chief. [The Indians] kept moving north and made their prisoners work with their squaws, hoeing corn and chopping wood. The prisoners got to running away so they made each prisoner lay at night between two Indians. My grandfather and one man were all there were left and they gave them no privileges, but they got together and made arrangements to go on a certain night and tucked food into their clothes to last them on their journey. They asked for the privilege to go to the door one night and when they got there they jumped for their lives. The Indians stood at the door with their guns and fired after them as they ran. They travelled all night and slept the rest of the day, and in three days got to Quebec, where they gave themselves up as prisoners to the French, and soon got exchanged to the English. While with the Indians, [my grandfather] got a stomach ache and the old chief buckled his belt onto him. At Quebec, it was taken away from him by French soldiers.

My grandfather lost two brothers in the French War. The Indians, when the war wound up, opened their bowels. Dr. Riken said to me that he saw one of the brothers, who had been served in this way, go some distance holding onto his bowels.

My grandfather was a pious man – always a bible with him wherever he went. He was small, but very spry stepping. He lived with his children and travelled a good deal from one child to another, and when stopping to rest would have his Bible out and read.

The Bell's Seasoning Story

William Bell's story is not unusual. In fact, abduction of colonial Americans by Native Americans was quite common in the first half of the 18th century, particularly at times of war, which were, in one form or another, frequent almost to the point of being continuous. It is sobering to think of the lives of our pioneer ancestors, tempered as they were by labor, the recurring demands of nature, and the threat of danger, and it is not surprising that, formed by such experience, souls like William Bell kept the Good Book near their breasts.

William survived to tell the tale and, perhaps, to see the founding of the new nation. We know that one of his sons, Joshua, did not, and another, Jonathan, was thrust into manhood on a hill called Breed's. Hugh, brother to Joshua and Jonathan and father to Robert Gibson, was born in 1770 and, thus, too young to go to war. His brothers, however, no doubt traded overalls and hay forks for uniforms and guns on little notice and traveled south seventy miles to Boston.

Boston lay restive and uneasy until April 19, 1775 and the first military conflicts of the war erupted at Lexington and Concord. Tensions built for almost two months. Three miles west, on the evening of June 16, the Colonial troops were mustered at Cambridge Common. Jonathan and Joshua Bell must have felt conflicting surges of excitement and fear. Then, on the evening of the 16th, under the command of Colonel William Prescott and the cover of darkness, they marched across Cambridge, down Charlestown Neck and, through the night, applied their youthful vigor to the hasty construction of breastworks and redoubt. At dawn, from their promontory, the young Bells would have seen the sparkling harbor, the city of Boston, and enemy warships. What must they have thought? There was little time for it. In the early morn, the sloop-of-war, *Lively*, began probing cannon fire. The war was on. Robert Gibson Bell describes the action, as told him by his uncle, Jonathan.

My uncle was in the Battle of Bunker Hill – he was only sixteen. A stranger who stood next to him was very friendly and told him how to stand and gave him other advice. Later, the man's head was shot off. [William adds that this was Asa Pollard, the first man killed in the battle.] When the man was killed, Jonathan could not help screaming. An officer, Colonel Prescott, shook his sword at him and said, "Not a word." After that he was as cool as any of them.

William, born in 1839, would have been just three-years-old when the Bunker Hill Monument was completed in 1842, and four when it was dedicated a year later and formed a grand staging to the luminous words of Daniel Webster.

The colonists of English America were of the people, and the people already free. They were of the middle, industrious and already prosperous class...among whom liberty first revived and respired, after a sleep of a thousand years, in the bosom of the dark ages...

Imagine how Webster, and the silent, towering monument for which he spoke, played upon the hearts of those in attendance.

The Bunker Hill Monument is finished. Here it stands. Fortunate in the high natural eminence on which it is placed – higher, infinitely higher in its objects and purpose, it rises over the land and over the sea, and visible at their homes to three hundred thousand of the People of Massachusetts, – it stands, a memorial of the last, and a monitor to the present, and to all succeeding generations…It has a purpose…That purpose enrobes it with dignity and moral grandeur [and] causes us to look up to it with a feeling of awe.

News of the day was careful to describe the presence of a dwindled formation of ancient men in their military regalia. Among them was Jonathan Bell, aged 82.

CHAPTER 4

The Early Years, 1857-1860

"Came to Boston in May, 1857 and began work with Seth F. Burt at 24 Quincy Market in the pork business with whom I remained for 4 years."

From the journal of William G. Bell

When William first explored the markets of Boston, he would have encountered a welter of sights and sounds. The epicenter of merchant activity, and especially the grocery trade, was the Quincy Market complex. Then, as today, it consisted of three parallel structures of brick and stone. Each is approximately 535 feet in length and 75 feet wide. The roofs are center peaked. The Quincy Market building, which occupies the center position, strikes a grand posture in Greek revival style, with four massive Doric pillars at its east and west ends and a soaring copper-based dome. Built in 1825, it is made mostly of New England granite.

Today the Quincy Market is a major tourist attraction and hosts eclectic retail offerings from Coach, Godiva and Victoria's Secret to Harley-Davidson and the Museum of Fine Arts. Year-round, it pulses with a sprawling diversity of energy and commerce. In that respect, it remains unchanged - in most other ways, the Quincy Market of William's era was a different world.

In the 1820s, Boston's population began to swell, as the city absorbed the first wave of European immigration. From around 40,000 souls in 1820, the population exploded to over four times that number, 170,000, by 1860, a year before the Wm. G. Bell Co. was established. In this era, Irish immigrants were the most abundant - as many as 35,000 had clambered ashore by 1850. By the waning years of the 19th century, as the family business approached its 40th anniversary, the city's burgeoning population has surged past half a million. By then, its crammed neighborhoods - North, West, and South ends - reverberated with the faces, language, food, clothing and religions of Irish, Germans, Lebanese, Syrians, French Canadians, Poles and Russians, many of whom sought work and opportunity on the docks and in the markets.

The Quincy Market of 1857, the year William arrived in the service of Seth Burt, proprietor, was a cacophony of sensory stimulation. Imagine the racket of barking vendors, wagon wheels on cobbled stones, livestock. Or the odor of fish, meat, and manure mingled with the aroma of fresh bread, fruits and spices. Or the sight of coal fires and steam in the cold, ships' masts, and the motley blending of vest-suited business men, stevedores, and butchers.

Two-hundred-year-old cobblestones were blanketed in an accretion of hay, dirt, discarded produce, and the ubiquitous pigeon droppings. Vendors opened stalls in the dull twilight between dark and gaslamp. Rough-hewn stalls spilled open to display every kind of durable and non-durable goods that could be purchased, grown, or caught around the world and hauled off the docks a stone's throw east. Cats, dogs, chickens, goats, mice, and pigeons – everywhere pigeons.

The markets formed a robust ballast for the splaying arms of docks that stretched east into Boston Harbor. The grandest of them, Long Wharf, not 100 feet from the eastern-most stalls, reached a quarter mile toward the sea and beckoned seafaring vessels to bring their goods to port.

The strip of cobblestones between dock and market formed the foot of Commercial Street, which curved to the northeast, hugged the harbor shoreline and formed a broad shoulder that supported the wharfs above Long Wharf - Commercial, Lewis, Union, Lincoln, Battery and more. Commercial Street continued on, as it does to this day, to enclose the top of the North End at the base of the colonial graveyard and Snow Hill. It hemmed in a neighborhood of narrow streets, ancient clapboard houses, including Paul Revere's, the Old North Church, and cramped, red brick tenements that spilled their occupants to the very edge of the market district.

This geography would form the daily world of William from his arrival in the employ of Mr. Burt in 1857 until the week of his death in 1915.

William had not arrived in Boston unprepared. At age 18, he came armed with big dreams and solid references. His former employer, Selwin Bancroft, vouched for him this way:

April 20th, 1857

To Seth F. Burt, Boston:

The bearer, ("Billy," as we all call him) William Bell, is a youth for whom I would gladly speak a word of commendation. I have carefully watched his movements for months, and can bear testimony to his good business habits. He is <u>industrious</u>, <u>pleasant</u> <u>and</u> <u>accommodating</u> <u>at</u> <u>all</u> <u>times</u>; and I am sure he will meet with favour and success wherever he may be known. If you need his help, take him by all means. If you don't, lend him a helping hand.

Yours, truly

Selwin Bancroft

Mr. Bancroft proved to be a good judge of character and William set out on a path that would validate Bancroft's prediction about "favour and success". We don't know much about the four years William worked for Mr. Burt, except that he was immersed in the preparation and trade of pork, was certainly observing and absorbing business skills and practices, and growing in maturity.

In September, 1857, the rest of William's family moved to the city of Charlestown. Geographically, Charlestown forms a kind of mirror image of the North End. It is directly to the north across the mouth of the Charles River. It is compact and built on and around the famous twin hills named Breed's and Bunker. In other ways, the neighborhood was distinctly different. It boasted broader thoroughfares and sturdy rows of spacious brick homes, some nestled around the old colonial center near Winthrop Square, others spreading out Main and High streets and up the steep hillsides toward the Bunker Hill Monument, a 221-foot Quincy granite obelisk completed just fifteen years earlier. The

The Bell's Seasoning Story

Warren Street and Charles Route bridges traversed the river and conveyed traffic to and from Boston. Quincy Market lay about a mile to the south.

Robert and Sophronia (Bruce) Bell and the twins, Abbie and Albert, aged 15, settled into temporary accommodations at High and Green Streets, in the shadow of Bunker Hill, where Robert's uncles had entered adulthood under the cannon and musket-fire of the British. Although they would occupy a total of five short-term residences in Charlestown over the next few years, the Bells had given William a place to call home.

Charlestown would play an important and colorful role in William's life over the next twenty years. It is charming to think that, in those early years, the young merchant might have unwittingly passed, perhaps tipping his hat, a demure Mary Whitney, whose own home was just a stroll from Winthrop Square.

CHAPTER 5

The William G. Bell Company

In 1861, at the age of twenty-two, William founded the company that bears his name. Records indicate that William's brother, Albert, aged nineteen, joined him as a partner in the business either at the start, or soon after.

In the company's earliest years, the brothers focused on grocery and market store provisions. Although the company's seasoning would one day eclipse this part of the business, the William G. Bell Company expanded its line of supplies and furnishings to include refrigerators, cutlery, bone cutters, scales, sausage fillers, and an alphabet of other food industry supplies.

William and Albert displayed the inexhaustible industry of youth. They built trade relationships, took on a growing line of brands, and even conducted business travel. Receipts and correspondence describe the expanding array of business activity. One is from the McCray Refrigerator Co., of Kendallville, Ind. Another from Wilson Brothers Grinding Mills, of Easton, Penn. Stevens' Butcher Supplies, Toledo, Ohio; Central Park Pickle Works, Manhattan, New York; Kansas City Packing Company; and many more.

Apart from this, there is little else in the records that chronicles the expansion and growth of the Bell brothers' enterprises. Perhaps the pace of their ambition simply didn't allow for any casual reflection. There is a hint from the future. An article written in 1909 tantalizingly recounts the "early years" of the company this way: "Some of the long-hour, hard-work, quick-change stunts of the youthful proprietors were a caution." We know nothing more.

Then, in 1867, Bell's Spiced Seasoning was born. One family legend has William learning the recipe at the apron strings of his mother, Sophronia. This excerpt from an article gives us a romantic description of its origins. "It was Mr. Bell's conception...the child of his brain. It belongs to just such properties as are handed down from generation to generation as family inheritances." In any case, an exotic blend of herbs and spices emerged from the culinary, not to mention the business, imagination of the Wm. G. Bell Co.

It was not to be the only seasoning. Over the years, many other seasonings were added, including Frankfurt seasoning, White German sausage seasoning, Brewster seasoning, XXX sausage seasoning, and New England Classic seasoning.

Yet, from early on, the Bell's Spiced Seasoning brand was the rising star. Perhaps it was the timing. The introduction of Bell's Spiced Seasoning coincided with the early years of a national Day of Thanksgiving to be celebrated on the final Thursday in November. Although described as a seasoning for "meats, game, fish & poultry," it has, from early on, been linked inseparably to the Thanksgiving turkey.

Among the company's inner circle, there was a sense of urgency about guarding the secrecy of the Bell's Spiced Seasoning recipe. After all, it was trumpeted in triumphal terms. "Bell's is the original. It's the alpha and omega. It came first, and will be when others won't be." The press even picked up on the recipe's secrecy, like a legend of old. One article reports, "At one time in the firm's history, when days were dark, rival manufacturers sought to secure the secret and carefully guarded formulas of the spiced seasoning." Years on, William wrote on the inside cover of his secret recipe book:

> To my son Alfred W. Bell in case of my death. The information herein contained should be guarded with great care remembering that no one has the secrets except your grandfather and the faithful Lilly, who has been with us since a young girl, now more than 18 years, and has always been faithful and true.

> Boston, July 8th 1892

The William G. Bell Company

Bell's Spiced Seasoning continued to grow in reputation and demand. To this day, the secret recipe book remains in loyal hands.

Chapter 6

Push, Pluck and Principle

Early on in William's scrapbook, he has mounted, one below the next, three letters from Everett National Bank. The first is dated January 14, 1879. William has written on it, in pencil, "age 40." The letter informs William that he has been elected to the Board of Directors. The second, dated October 28, 1890, reads, "I am very sorry to learn of your travails. I wish I could give you strength to equal your needs. I would do so quickly and at whatever sacrifice to my own self." The letter is signed, "Your friend, Warren Sawyer," the bank's president. The third, dated November 8, 1890, informs him that "the resignation of William G. Bell [as a Director] has been accepted."

What happened? And why are events as late as 1890 placed so early in William's journal, alongside mementos of some of his earliest successes?

Then, some forty pages later, the matter is revealed. There we find an article from the Boston Herald entitled, "THE FINANCES OF BELL & CO, Assignee Hinckley Submits Statement to Creditors." On November 5, 1890 the Wm. G. Bell Co. and its co-partners, William G. Bell and Albert D. S. Bell, filed for bankruptcy protection.

I can guess at the placement of the letters so early in William's documents. Among the most hallowed memories family members had of William, spoken in hushed tones, was the one that he had paid back ever dollar owed to creditors after the bankruptcy, *even though the law did not require it.* This life lesson was impressed upon the whole family, and echoed down the generations.

The details form a clear picture: the company had over-extended itself, primarily in real estate, some of which had nothing to do with its provisions and seasoning business.

More than 70 creditors filled the Parker House hall to listen to the details of the Bells' bankruptcy. In all, the debts exceeded half a million dollars – more than $12 million today. Many of the debts reflect the rapid growth of a company whose assets stretched from Sargent's Wharf in Boston to shares in the Kansas City Packing Company, Kansas City, Missouri.

One item, in particular, stood out from the rest. It is a mortgage for 189 acres of land on Hough's Neck, in Quincy, some thirteen miles to the southeast of Boston. Surrounded by the waters of greater Boston Harbor, Hough's Neck was being developed as a summer retreat for affluent Bostonians. The Bell's Manet Land Company had already invested in a street railway which shuttled residents from the Old Colony line in Quincy.

As is so often true in real estate, there were high hopes for a profitable future. The Herald article says of the Bell's Hough's Neck investment, "Their present holdings are considerable, and if they realize all they hope, the actual showing of assets will be better than it now appears." The Hough's Neck property is never again mentioned in William's papers.

Another article states that "an investigating committee reports that no evidence of dishonesty has been found."

One article concludes:

> Mr. William G. Bell called on his brother last evening and found him prostrated. He had been under a tremendous strain for a long time before the failure, as he was the financial manager…He is spoken of as a generous-hearted man, and he keenly feels the blow to the firm.
>
> Mr. William G. Bell gave his attention to the store and to the provisions business.

Bad news travels quickly and far. There was a prolific outpouring of support and sympathy for the brothers. William kept many of these, mostly from a wide assortment of business and professional colleagues. However, two letters are unique and noteworthy. One relates that its signers "sympathise with you most sincerely." It continues, "You have always been most kind and indulgent employers and if we can, at this time, help you in any way, we will most gladly do so." It is signed by sixteen employees of the Wm. G. Bell Co.

The other is written on Howard University letterhead in the hand of Rev. Jeremiah E. Rankin, President. He writes:

My Dear Christian Brother:

I have just seen notice of the great financial sorrow which has overtaken you. I need not tell you and your dear wife how great is our sympathy, & how sincere is our prayer that the One, who can make all things work together for good to us, will be very gracious and tender to you.

With love to you all,

Affectionately yours,

J. E Rankin

Reverend Rankin, the well-known civil rights leader, had been a dear friend of William's father, Robert.

It is symbolic, and typical of William's personality, that mounted just below the bankruptcy papers was an article entitled, "SUCCEED AFTER FAILURE, Great Business Men Who Failed But Never Gave Up."

The Wm. G. Bell Co. shook off the failure of 1890 and achieved a new chapter of success. It seems Rev. Rankin's prayer was answered.

Chapter 7

Albert D. S. Bell

The traumatic bankruptcy marked the end of Albert D. S. Bell's participation in the family business. Perhaps it is poetic justice that he went on to considerable success in the real estate business.

Albert was an early developer of the Chestnut Hill area. A quaint colonial village, by the 1870s Chestnut Hill had become one of the premier new suburban developments. Frederick Law Olmsted, the legendary landscape architect, had already designed the 135-acre Chestnut Hill Reservoir, as well as the serene Commonwealth Avenue, which arced gracefully west just to the south of Albert's home.

That historic boulevard was a labor of love for Albert. He, Judge Lowell and others presented the first plan to the city of Newton for a comprehensive system of boulevards, of which Commonwealth Avenue became the crown jewel – a sylvan necklace stretching from Lake Street (at present-day Boston College) in the east to Auburndale in the west.

On Chestnut Hill, home for Albert and his growing family was a gracious colonial manor at the crest of a hill on Ward and Hammond Streets. King's Handbook of Newton (1889) provides this description:

Near the end of Hammond Street is Waban Hill, rising to a height of 313 feet, and supporting on its side the smooth green embankments of the Newton reservoir. Higher up, the road reaches the grassy summit, from which is outspread a view of amazing grandeur, including Wachusett and Monadnock [Author's note: Mountains, some 40 and 70 miles, respectively, to the northwest] in the blue distance...Across the valley, Waltham, Watertown, Arlington Heights, Mount Auburn, Cambridge, and the great Memorial Hall tower [at Harvard University]. Farther around extend the long brick vistas of Boston, with the conspicuous towers of Trinity and the Old South [churches at Copley Square], and the glittering State House dome; and beyond stretches the wide blue plain of the open sea, flecked with white sails. The Blue Hills close the magnificent panorama on the southeast and the fair foreground is dotted with the villas and estates and villages of Newton. This view has been pronounced by travelers the finest of all the suburbs in Boston, so famous for their hilltop prospects of sea and cities and mountains.

Not long after this description was written, Albert moved his family across the Charles River valley to Cambridge, where he lived, at 164 Brattle Street, until his death in 1908.

Brattle Street in the 1890s probably resembled itself today, with stately colonial and Victorian homes, spread comfortably along the tree-lined great-road between Harvard Square and Watertown. What had begun as a cart and cow path between the colonial settlements of "New Towne" and Watertown, had taken on an historic prominence as "Tory Row" before the Revolution. Best known today as the address of

Longfellow's house, Brattle Street, in the words of Harvard historian Samuel Eliot, is "one of the most beautiful and one of the most historic streets in America."

The Longfellow house epitomizes the atmosphere of Brattle Street – pedigree, privilege, and learning – and must have been infectious to Albert and his growing family. The Bell children would have routinely rounded the bend at Sparks Street and passed the home of the famous poet, occupied after his death in 1882 by his eldest daughter, Alice.

> Between the dark and the daylight,
>   When the night is beginning to lower,
> Comes a pause in the day's occupations,
>   That is known as the Children's Hour.
>
> I hear in the chamber above me
>   The patter of little feet,
> The sound of a door that is opened,
>   And voices soft and sweet.
>
> From my study I see in the lamplight,
>   Descending the broad hall stair,
> Grave Alice, and laughing Allegra,
>   And Edith with golden hair.

Albert's days at the Wm. G. Bell Co. were over, but his family's accomplishments were just begun. He married Susan Laura Stoughton of Chester, Vermont and had six children: Laura, Stoughton, Gertrude, Conrad, Gibson, Hugh, and Stuart. Their home on Brattle Street was fondly remembered by William's granddaughter, Dorothy, who, as an elderly lady, recounted exuberant dancing in the ballroom at her cousins' home.

Albert would remain active in his church, civics, and business. However, another aspect of his industry also shines forth. Like his brother, Albert has ceased formal education at an early age. There is no record that he attended any academic institution after age fourteen. This did not stop his intellectual imagination, and he became an avid book collector, as attested to in this excerpt from an article in the Boston Evening Transcript:

To the book collector there are few works of greater interest than book catalogues, especially if they be of old or remarkable collections...Three such catalogues, from the Napoleonic collection of Mr. A. D. S. Bell of Cambridge, are a treasured part of that splendid lot of books and prints which he has formed in years of pursuit....The catalogues themselves are rare items these days, and are literally worth their weight in gold.

Albert died on February 7, 1908, at the age of sixty-six. The Boston Budget The Beacon ran a cover photograph and caption, "The Late A. D. S. Bell. A Much Beloved Bostonian." Perhaps the most appropriate reminiscence came from the New England Grocer:

We remember Mr. Bell especially as he was when associated with his brother, William G. Bell...In those days, it was our privilege to see him often...His greeting was always kindly. He was sympathetic, reasonable in his judgment...These traits were as prominent in his relations with the humblest employee as with the most prominent person...

Albert died seven years before his older brother, who, at age sixty-nine, still had the energy and ambition of men half his age.

Chapter 8

The Dean of Boston Business

A serpentine sward, punctuated with the concrete warp and weave of surface streets and tunnels, now occupies what used to be 48-54 Commercial Street. This urban greenery is a vast improvement over the girdered monstrosity of the elevated central artery that slashed through Boston for decades.

Just over a century ago, industry buzzed at this address. After 50 years in business, the Wm. G. Bell Co. was prospering. The Butchers' and Packers' Gazette wrote with unrestrained admiration. "A visit to the establishment of the Wm. G. Bell Co., 48-54 Commercial Avenue [sic. Street], Boston, Mass. will surprise when the full extent and ramifications of the business are considered." They describe the diverse lines of products, including patented sausage bags of Irish linen, a large line of butchers' and grocery fixtures, McCray refrigerators, and, of course, seasonings and spices.

The Gazette article continues, "...for upwards of fifty years the members of the Bell family have attended to the weighing and mixing of the herbs and spices," and "the output exceeds six thousand cans daily."

Three blocks north, at 209-211 North Street, a crooked corner from Paul Revere's house, more Bell activity could be found. Here, the Gazette reports, "bales of herbs and spices are stored...Here will also be found the mills for grinding the sweet herbs and spices which enter into the manufacture of 'Bell's Spiced Seasoning.'"

The Gazette delights in the technology and statistics that describe the productivity.

The product is transferred to a diamond-shaped mixer holding about 300 pounds, which revolves 33 revolutions a minute...The seasoning is carefully pressed into each can and weighed and packed into round trays holding 70 cans each. It requires 300 trays that hold 21,000 cans.

The article's piece de resistance? "The firm uses over 2 million cans per year."

By 1911, when this article was published, the William G. Bell Company was approaching its zenith. The ascent would continue until his brief illness and death on October 27, 1915, aged 76 years, 8 months and 26 days.

William had built a business that was a mercantile reflection of himself – hardworking, efficient, and fair. The Boston Budget and Beacon called him "the dean of Boston businessmen who personally direct their own affairs." Such a business profited from William's personal vision and energy, but also, in later days, would suffer from his sudden departure.

One could not paint a better picture of the 'dean' and his business than did a temporary employee, who wrote this charming missive in July, 1907 (on The William G. Bell Company stationery).

The Dean of Boston Business

July 25, 1907

My Dear Fred:

Monday, while busy at my own office, I received a call to go to The William G. Bell Company, 48-52 Commercial Street and I came here to work on Tuesday morning. It is only for this week and I shall be sorry when Saturday comes. I question if there is another business house like it in Boston. You know in twenty-one years of business life I have seen many business men and business methods and here both are ideal. The business is large and to give you some idea of it I will quote a sentence from a letter which Mr. Bell dictated to me. "If we were to quote you prices on all the different goods we carry we should have to make quotations on more than 2,000 different articles." My letters have been on refrigerators, meat knives and blocks, coffee mills, oil pumps, lard pails, advertising, labels, spices – as this is the house that makes the famous poultry seasoning – and many other subjects...The young ladies in the office are exceptionally pleasant and remarkably efficient. The store is neat and attractive and the clerks and salesmen are gentlemanly and seem to take as much interest to see that all goes well as Mr. Bell himself. This can be explained by something Mr. Bell said today when we were talking about wages.

He said, "I always aim to see how <u>much</u> I can pay a man, not how <u>little</u>;" and this is true also of the business, as is shown in his correspondence; he aims to see how much he can give his customer for his money, not how little.

I presume you will think me enthusiastic over the place. Well, I am. I have talked about it at home all the week, as well as wondered at it. All is so harmonious and everyone is so efficient! No profanity, no cross words, no jealousy, no shirking, nothing done when Mr. Bell is out that would not be done if he was here, everything done by every employee as if the business were his or her own!

Promptly at eight o'clock everyone and everything starts in motion and kept in motion until five o'clock – no rush or confusion, only everyone part of a system, which system reflects the man at the head of it all, the President of the Company, Mr. William G. Bell. He is the most remarkable man! Usually I can guess a person's age but I judged him to be sixteen years younger than he really is. He is a typical old-school <u>gentleman</u> – one of that rare type seldom seen in these days of "frenzied" money-getting, - particular as to his personal appearance, considerate of others, kindly, courteous, polished and refined in his manner, possessed of a remarkable sense of humor, yet withal dignified. He is a fluent talker – very much too fluent for the ordinary stenographer (I was number six in one week, and only his kind indulgence allowed me to remain the last, as he talked many times faster than I could write, especially about Freeze-em, Iceine, Zanzibar Liquid Ham Smoke, etc.) – a man with a remarkable command of language and a grasp of the detail connected with his business which is really almost incredible. Everything seems to be systematically arranged in his mind, not one fact or one detail lost sight of or forgotten. He is a most remarkable man and no one can be in his employ and not improve in business capacity, mentally, morally, and physically. Presume you wonder at this last, but even with all the business cares and worries he has on his mind he has time and thought to spare on a little joke, some fact to interest or instruct, or a word of good advice to give. He seems interested in everything about his employees and always ready with some helpful or wise or appreciative word. He says, "My people seldom leave my employ," and I do not wonder.

I read, the other day, a little story of Abraham Lincoln. At one time in Washington, Mr. Lincoln passed some friends and associates on the street. They turned and watched him as he walked away and one of them remarked to his friend, "There goes a man!"

The same might be said of Mr. Bell, for he is in every way "a man."

I have often said, "I have yet to see an ideal man," but I can't say it again for I have seen him in Mr. Bell and I shall always remember this week's experience and be better for it. One could not become a part of this establishment for a day without being "larger" at night.

I must close. Mr. Bell will shortly return from lunch, and then more letters – no social ones, although to all his customers he writes in a friendly tone that <u>must</u> impress them.

Yours, as usual,

Etta B.

It is a tad melodramatic, no doubt, but reflect for a moment on the circumstances. A veteran woman in the workplace who has spent two days, plus the morning hours of Thursday, in William's employ. She has logged twenty-one years in a man's world, and responds with a flood of unbridled admiration and gratitude, when the first opportunity can be stolen, for fair and honorable treatment.

At this high-water mark, Bell's had established success and renown. An impressive array of chefs and dining establishments served up glowing praise for the now famous spiced seasoning.

Your dressing merits all that you claim for it…The satisfaction of having it at all times is apparent to any chef du cuisine.

F. E. Balch, Steward
Memorial Hall, Harvard College

I have been over-persuaded to try other makes. In every instance I have been obliged to throw them away and fall back on the old reliable Bell's Spiced Poultry Seasoning.

J. B. Wistar, Steward
Grand Central Hotel, New York City

I beg to say that I have used Bell's Spiced Seasoning for a great many years in the various hotels which I have conducted, and, in my opinion, it is the best mixture that has ever been put on the market…It has never failed to give entire satisfaction. It is the most superior article of its kind in use.

Allen Ainslee, Esq., President
Hotel Lenox, Boston

The Bell's Seasoning Story

I have used your spiced seasoning several years and cheerfully recommend it.

Joseph Beckman
Parker House, Boston

While this applause appears somewhat provincial, similar praise is received from Chicago, Milwaukee, St. Augustine, Atlanta, even Japan.

There was even cause for some self-congratulations:

A Spicy Orchestra.

Bell's Spiced Seasoning gives the Turkey proper tone. No other spiced seasoning can make Turkey Dressing so delicious and delicate; so snappy and pungent. If all the Turkeys that have been seasoned with Bell's Spiced Seasoning in the past 35 years could be arranged in orchestral parade, they would fill the air with spicy music that would be "heard round the world."

Chapter 9

Adventures and Controversies

Family papers reflect the many layers of
William's character: boyish and energetic,
almost perpetual in his curiosity about
business; somewhat puritanical about big
picture stuff like Catholic education and
temperance; practical and generous in personal
relations. In October, 1914, The Boston Budget
and Beacon reported it this way:

Like all strong characters, Mr. Bell has made
some enemies, but his friends love him for the
enemies he has made, and now at seventy-five,
broadminded, upright, shrewd, – he enjoys the
esteem of the community and the prospect of many
more years of usefulness.

Another notice of praise, this one from his Congregational parish, The Second Church in Newton, hints at William's capacity for well-intentioned controversy. The Reverend John Edgar Park writes:

> While kind and charitable, he was also fearless of wrong-doers, and no public evil could exist in the community without instant and vigorous action on his part to abolish it…"

These qualities can be seen in a number of episodes in William's adult life. One can imagine where such heart-felt and head-strong activism might lead in a city that was percolating with religious, ethnic and cultural change.

The Curious Case of Philip Friedrichs

A series of newspaper clippings and handwritten letters appears in William's scrapbook. They relate to a missing teenager named Philip Friedrichs, from New Orleans. The first entry, dated December 10, 1896, is entitled, "WAS IT FRIEDRICHS? Bell Thinks He Has Seen The New Orleans Runaway." The article describes the mysterious disappearance of the young man from his home in July of 1896. William, who had somehow followed the story "with great interest," said that a young man fitting Friedrichs' description entered his office late the previous afternoon, saying he was strapped for money and had eaten nothing the previous day. He gave the lad 50 cents for a night's lodging and dinner (around $13 today) and instructed him to return to the office the following morning.

The next day, the young man told William that he would like to get to Norwich, Conn., where he had a friend. William provided him with $2.50 (over $50 today) and instructed him to pay it back when his fortunes improved. Young Friedrichs went on his way, and William wrote to his parents in New Orleans to inform them of his encounter.

There follow two impassioned letters from Mrs. Friedrichs, thanking William for his generosity and advice. The second letter was dated March 9, 1897. Then, on September 23, 1903, William received a final letter. An elated Mrs. Friedrichs writes:

Dear Mr. Bell,

Never having forgotten your interest in the disappearance of my son, Philip Friedrichs, I write to inform you that, unexpectedly, he returned home today after an absence of seven years."

In an outbreak of adolescent independence, young Philip had left his traveling theatrical company and gone on a walkabout that included known stops in Boston and Chicago. We don't know if young Philip ever paid William back, but suspect that notice of his return home was recompense enough.

The Citizens' Law and Order League

By the 1880s, William found himself involved in a range of civic activities. Some, like acting as a Justice of the Peace, were practical duties. Others he immersed himself in with evangelical zeal, as exemplified by his participation in the Citizens' Law and Order League, which was committed to the control and restriction of alcoholic consumption to the fullest extent of the law. His clippings on the subject are copious, and include some colorful headlines and stories. To wit, "Reform Wave Strikes Newton. Police Hot After Druggists and Scorching Chauffeurs. Hunt For Drunks, Too."

The righteous passion of the League's adherents can be summed up in a letter from a Mr. A. S. Twombley.

> Dear Sir,
>
> I am sorry I cannot be with you at the meeting on Tuesday next, but I am obliged to attend the Commencement Exercises at Yale College.
>
> You need no assurance from me of my sympathy for your work – my hand, tongue & pen are yours at any time...
>
> The Liquor Business is well called "The Devil's Mill-Race;" let the Law and Order League confine it within the narrowest limits of the law. If we cannot prevent its turning the wheels of gin-mills, it must not overflow our fields and submerge our institutions."

So armed went William into the most raucous of the controversies he recorded.

In the fall of 1881, two forces intersected. One was the assassination and ultimate death of President Garfield on September 19, 1881.

The other was the "screen law" in Boston, which prohibited the covering of ground floor windows on establishments that served liquor. The scene was set.

Sometime between the death of the President and October 2nd, according to an article in the Saturday Evening Express, a number of pubs and taverns along Main Street in Charlestown hung "mourning embellishments and drapings" that were not in violation of the law. This arrangement, however, did not please William, who entered each establishment and demanded that the drapings be removed. Once rebuffed, he returned with a police officer, who enforced Bell's demand.

The press used its advantage to full effect, calling William a "religious crank," and a "pessimire of society" who "is a deacon on Sundays and peddles lard and pork weekdays." The article dripped with indignation. William "made his demands in a bombastic and arrogant way," it claimed, and wondered how long the saloon fraternity will tolerate such treatment. After all, "this is the second or third time [Bell] has invaded their domains." Not lacking for theatre, the author concluded, "In olden times, the pillory and whipping block was utilized for the benefit of a class of society of which this person Bell is so able a representative."

As previously reported, "Like all strong characters, Mr. Bell has made some enemies, but his friends love him for the enemies he has made."

A Letter from Prison in Spain

The era was not without its own brand of scams, or at least appeals of dubious authenticity. William has memorialized three in his scrapbook. The first begins, in a strong and hurried hand, with a flourish, "This letter will doubtless astonish you…" The author claims to be in jail in Madrid and speaks of portmanteaus, secrets, Mexican banks, and three concealed checks worth 120,000 pounds. The letter concludes with an urgent plea for William to contact a special confidant – "by cablegram, never a letter." Did the letter astonish William? We don't know, but apart from marking the date of its receipt, he gives no evidence of having benefitted from a sudden Spanish windfall.

We will never know what made William so alluring to prisoners of the former Spanish empire, but a year earlier, in October, 1905, he had received a sprawling narrative penned from "Castle fort of Barajas" – [Cartagena, Colombia]. The tale of woe is spun by a man with the illustrious and poetic name of "Estanislao Cortina." Once an important official in Spanish Cuba, he fell on the wrong side of the rebellion there and was captured, but not before secreting out 29,000 pounds, which he desperately wanted William to secure. The mechanism for doing so required secret passwords, clerical intermediaries, and, of course, William's bank information.

What was Senor Cortina's motive? He invoked the memory of his beloved wife, Mary Bell, and the care of their only daughter, the soon-to-be-orphaned Julia. Cortina's days were numbered, as he was "condemned to 18 years penal servitude." In return for the money, wouldn't William consent to be the guardian of his niece?

Once again, there is no evidence that William ever received any colonial treasure, and we know that his "niece," Julia, never appeared on the family stage.

Finally, we find a letter from M. Perlmutter from Jerusalem, Palestine. He describes the plight of his olive wood business. His wife and family are starving. "Please remember," he implores, "a poor and honest handicraftsman whose handicrafts express the fundamental principles of religion and humanity." He included a flower-album with Holy Land olive wood decorations. We do not know how much time had transpired when William replied on December 13, 1904, and enclosed $2.00.

Dear Sir,

If you and your family were in a starving condition when the little booklet was sent me, I fear you will all be in Heaven before this reaches Jerusalem. However, I presume you have left matters in such a way that the money will be cared for by your descendents, and they will most likely advise you of its receipt.

This one William deemed worthy of his charity, but not without a mild Yankee lecture.

The Protégé

There is another letter, written on letterhead, TUDHOPE & BORST, in a robust font above two stately engraved hens. It is dated December 16, 1907. In it, the writer, Thomas D. Borst, recalls that day, 28 years before, when he met William. It was on the Day Line Steamer Daniel Drew, going up the Hudson en route to Saratoga. At the time, Thomas was just fourteen years old. William had given him advice (about smoking cigarettes) and taken him under wing.

During their ensuing correspondence, William encouraged Thomas to spread his wings. So, Thomas left home, "entered your employ, and changed the entire course of my life." He concludes, "If I have accomplished anything worthwhile in all these years, it is to your credit and kindly efforts in my behalf."

Alongside his prodigious business output, William found time to show kindness and generosity, to reveal uprightness and shrewdness, to provoke enemies and kindle friends.

Chapter 10

An End So Sudden

Boston Daily Globe, October 28, 1915

WILLIAM G. BELL DEAD
Well-Known Boston Manufacturer Had Been Ill at
West Newton Home Since Saturday

NEWTON, Oct. 27 – William Gibson Bell, president
and general manager of the William G. Bell
Company of Boston...died shortly after 10 o'clock
this evening at his home, 49 Shaw St., West Newton,
where he had lived for the past 30 years.

On page 150 of his scrapbook, William pasted a
letter, dated September 22, 1915, which he had
received from William Easton of Wm. H Easton

& Co., Newport, Rhode Island. In it, Mr. Easton thanks William for his "very strong favorable endorsement of our firm," and that it was "most kind of you to speak so well of us."

On page 151, there is a Valentine card, "For Father," unsigned. Then the large, manila folio papers go blank.

On page 158 is pasted a death announcement from the Second Church in Newton:

October 27, 1915

William G. Bell died today, of pneumonia.

Just the year before, The Wm. G. Bell Co. had expanded its operations to include showrooms at 19-24 South Market, four floors of prominence at the Faneuil Hall end of the Quincy Market complex. Large American flags fluttered above the doors, and below the gold leaf signage, "THE WM. G. BELL CO."

Just the year before, The American Cultivator had finished its feature on William by describing him, "at seventy-five…the hardest worked man in his own company."

That same article began by calling William "the dean of Boston business men who *personally* direct their affairs." (Emphasis added.) It applauded the "early hours and many of them," and reported that "the morning finds him at his offices starting the day with an impetus that electrifies the entire corps."

How would the void be filled? Could it be filled? Could the company founded by him sixty-four years early, and vivified by him daily survive the loss of William?

Epilogue

The Waning Years

One can only imagine how William's family and business managed after his death. His company and his household were manifestations of his patriarchy. His good health and industry were evident just weeks before. There is no doubt, William did not expect to die, and it must have been a paralyzing shock for his family.

Had William stepped back from the business he founded, planned for succession, retired, then things might have turned out differently. Son Alfred, now age forty-six, had spent his adult life in the family business and home under the wing of his formidable father.

A notice posted soon after William's death declares:

ALFRED W. BELL AT THE HELM

Alfred W. Bell, son of William G. Bell, founder of the William G. Bell Co., has succeeded his father as manager of this big enterprise, the largest poultry dressing house in the world.

Alfred was a quiet, gentle man. He was strongly inclined toward the fine arts. He left many fine examples of artistic expression. (These include drawings of fishing craft and coastline, pastels of the skyline of Boston from his daughter's home in Winthrop, and an intricate New England barn and farm equipment, handmade with tiny pin-nails, clapboards, leather harnesses, metalwork, and mica windows.) Was he up to the challenge? Could he master the art of business? William must have known the temperament of his son, but did not expect the suddenness of his own demise.

He seems to have had plans for the continuation of Bell generations in the family enterprise. In May of 1914, William received a reply to a letter he had written to Mr. Hibbard, Principal of the Bryant & Stratton School, a business institute in Boston, to inquire about the progress of his grandson, William. Mr. Hibbard wrote that "your grandson's progress in this school is very satisfactory." Grandson William, my grandfather, was eighteen years old at the time. It is likely that his grandfather's death just over a year later affected his career path. He never did enter the family business.

By 1918, two events had occurred that marked the end of the business and family era begun by William almost sixty years earlier. The Wm. G. Co. he had begun with his brother, Albert, in 1861, was sold to the D & L Slade Co., an old Boston rival, and the big house at 49 Shaw Street, West Newton was sold, its furniture and keepsakes parceled, and its occupants scattered.

Perhaps it was time for the household to disband. Mary and William's daughter, Marion, was establishing her married life with husband, Douglas Crook. Son, Alfred, and his wife, Hattie, had been under the elders' roof all of their married life. Three of their four children were approaching adulthood. Only Douglas remained firmly in his youth.

Mary, William's widow, went west to Springfield as early as 1917, and lived out her life there in her daughter's home.

What happened to the Wm. G. Bell Co.? As we have seen, Alfred became manager of the company. Financial reports for years 1915-1918 indicate that the company's performance remained steady. However, behind the scenes, there must have been momentous discussions about its future. Family records do not shed light on the circumstances surrounding the company's sale to D&L Slade, but, by 1918 the two companies were combined and doing business at 189 State Street.

After the acquisition by D&L Slade, Alfred stayed on and was involved with the company until his death in 1950.

As the years ran on, Bell's Seasoning remained a New England favorite. In a 1983 article in the Boston Globe, Francis Brooks, a former president of the Bell's line, said that by the 1950s, "Bell's wagged the tail of the [Slade] dog."

The Waning Years

In 1972, Bell's was acquired by Brady Enterprises, Inc., in East Weymouth, Mass. For forty years, under the stewardship of the Brady family, Bell's Seasoning continued to flourish. Along the way, cooking icons Julia Child and Martha Stewart have expressed their devotion to the unique spiced seasoning – as have countless others, spread across continents, for whom Bell's Seasoning is a fragrant and delicious reminder of their New England home.

Postscript

The Women

Were it not for the women, there would have been no William G. Bell, no company in his name, no enduring brand, no descendant to write this book.

Sophronia Bruce

Born on December 30, 1807, in Acworth, New Hampshire, to Susanna Bruce (her family name also) and Joseph Bruce. Sophronia was the widow of Robert Doe, with whom she had a son, Joseph. Thus, Robert Gibson Bell was Sophronia's second husband.

Sophronia traveled far from her Bruce kin to accompany her husband. His occupation as a tanner took them to antebellum North Carolina before they settled into their golden years on Adams Street, Winter Hill, in Somerville. It is from there that Sophronia presided over a splendid 50th wedding anniversary in 1885.

There is a tender New Year card, dated Jan 2nd, 1879 from Sophronia. In a delicate, old-fashioned hand and old-world lilt, it reads:

My Dear Grand Child,
May the gentle gale of prosperity waft you smoothly down the stream of life; and may your latter days be as happy as your former days have been unhappy; those are the wishes of your
Dear Grand Mother – Sophronia Bell

I am the custodian of a formal oil painting of Sophronia, which was done from the photograph taken at the 50th anniversary celebration. In it, she looks determined but careworn, as if reflecting less the gaiety of the evening than the motherly duties of a lifetime.

Mary Hanson Goldsmith Whitney

Born January 26, 1842, in Boston. Mary was the daughter of Anna Hooper Goldsmith and Alfred Whitney, of Charlestown. She grew up on the shoulder of Bunker Hill in a charming brick townhouse. Her beloved big brother, George, died of typhus at age 19, when Mary was sixteen. Mary's mother, Anna, came from the North Shore branch of colonial "come-overers", and had a rich family history in Manchester, Ipswich, and other villages and towns north of Boston.

Alfred, her dad, was a merchant in Boston, selling lamp and gas fixtures from his firm Whitney & Tappan, on Winter Street. He was descended from John and Elinor Whitney of Watertown, famous among early colonial progenitors.

An oil painting of Mary reveals large, smoky eyes. Do they betray a more exotic strain in her ancestry than her staid Boston circumstances describe? There are Goldsmiths and Kitfields (Kuitveals) in her lineage, and stories to be discovered in her face.

Hattie Gertrude Johnson

Born September 12, 1869, in Holliston, Massachusetts. She had a large clan of Johnsons, Parkers, Hawkes and other relations in Holliston, whose birthdates crowd the town records and headstones the Holliston cemetery. She lived in the shadows of her parents-in-law at the big house on Shaw Street and, according to her youngest son, my Great Uncle Doug, found joy and contentment in her own home in the Newton Highlands.

I gleaned the most about her from Great Uncle Doug, who adored her. I imagine that his gentle, kind, lyrical spirit and sparkling turn of phrase he inherited from her, or learned at her knee.

Susan Laura Stoughton

Born July 16, 1844 in Chester, Vermont to Laura Elmira Clark and Henry Evander Stoughton. The Stoughtons were a prominent Vermont family. Susan's brother, Edwin, was a Brigadier General in the Union Army and earned both infamy and shame as the embarrassed captive of Confederate cavalry legend, Colonel Mosby. She, like the other women featured here, left her ancestral home to provide the maternal foundation her growing family needed, and, in doing so, receded from view.

I am sorry that they play such a small part in this book: one completely unrepresentative of their actual contribution to the lives and fortunes described.

Finis

ABOUT THE AUTHOR

David N. Bell has deep roots in Massachusetts soil. He grew up in Cohasset, and has the ocean in his veins. He attended Haverford College, outside of Philadelphia, and received his M.B.A. from the Wharton School at the University of Pennsylvania.

David has managed his own food and nutrition consulting practice for many years. However, it is the excitement of family life, past and present, that keeps him feeling youthful.

David lives in New Bedford, Massachusetts with his wife and ever-changing combinations of their six children.

CPSIA information can be obtained
at www.ICGtesting.com
Printed in the USA
LVOW11s0229080817
544214LV00001B/8/P